EAVESDROPPING ON ELEPHANTS

HOW LISTENING HELPS CONSERVATION

PATRICIA NEWMAN

MILLBROOK PRESS • MINNEAPOLIS

FOR JOE, FOR OBVIOUS REASONS

Acknowledgments: With profound thanks to the forward-thinking staff of The Elephant Listening Project at Cornell University's Lab of Ornithology—Katy Payne, founding member, former director, and acoustic biologist; Peter Wrege, director and behavioral ecologist; Andrea Turkalo, founding member and biologist with the Wildlife Conservation Society (retired); Liz Rowland, research analyst; Daniela Hedwig, postdoctoral research fellow; and Anahita Verahrami, research assistant. Additional thanks to documentary film director Todd McGrain for sharing Sesélé's quotes and to my daughter, Elise Newman Montanino, for introducing me to ELP when she worked there as an undergraduate.

Text copyright © 2019 by Patricia Newman

Millbrook Press
A division of Lerner Publishing Group, Inc.
241 First Avenue North
Minneapolis, MN 55401 USA

For reading levels and more information, look up this title at www.lernerbooks.com.

Main body text set in Adrianna 12/19.
Typeface provided by Chank.

For more digital content, download a QR code reader app on your tablet or other smart device. Then scan the QR codes throughout the book to see and hear elephants in action.

Library of Congress Cataloging-in-Publication Data

Names: Newman, Patricia, 1958– author.
Title: Eavesdropping on elephants : how listening helps conservation / Patricia Newman.
Description: Minneapolis : Millbrook Press, [2018] | Audience: Ages 9–14. | Audience: Grades 4 to 6. | Includes bibliographical references and index.
Identifiers: LCCN 2017053300 (print) | LCCN 2017059854 (ebook) | ISBN 9781541524743 (eb pdf) | ISBN 9781541515710 (lb : alk. paper)
Subjects: LCSH: African elephant—Behavior—Juvenile literature. | African elephant—Central African Republic—Juvenile literature. | Animal communication—Juvenile literature. | African elephant—Conservation—Juvenile literature.
Classification: LCC QL737.P98 (ebook) | LCC QL737.P98 N44 2018 (print) | DDC 599.67/4—dc23

LC record available at https://lccn.loc.gov/2017053300

Manufactured in the United States of America
1-44277-34454-4/4/2018

CONTENTS

Mother elephants travel in the forest with their calves, but they use clearings to reconnect with grandparents, aunts, nieces, nephews, and cousins.

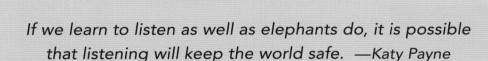

FOREST RUMBLES

If we learn to listen as well as elephants do, it is possible that listening will keep the world safe. —Katy Payne

THE AIR VIBRATES WITH DEEP RUMBLES THAT THUNDER LIKE A BASS DRUM.

In a tropical forest clearing in the Central African Republic, families of forest elephants flap their ears and smell the ground with their trunks. High-pitched screams and trumpet blasts accompany deep roars. Many overlapping voices—some high, some low—broadcast the news. A male and female have just mated. Grandmothers, aunts, cousins, nephews, nieces, and even complete strangers twirl in circles to show their excitement.

Soon other elephant families enter the clearing. They too rumble and roar to play their part in this symphony of sound. The clearing echoes with the overlapping harmonies of simultaneous elephant calls.

Do you wonder what they're saying to one another?

Scientists from the Elephant Listening Project do. They eavesdrop on endangered African forest elephants not only to figure out what they're saying but also to save them from extinction.

Forest elephants make the music of the forest possible. As a keystone species, their daily activity helps the forest flourish. Without elephants, many of the animals and plants of the forest wouldn't exist. As elephants wander in search of food, they create miles of crisscrossing trails between the great trees and through the tangle of vines and brush. Bush pigs, buffalo, bongos, gorillas, and even people use these trails. The elephants' bulky bodies flush out insects and small reptiles that birds eat. Their agile trunks pump high pressure jets of water underground to mine for the precious salt that all animals need to survive. And they eat fruit and spread the seeds through their feces so new trees grow. Saving forest elephants saves the forest and its inhabitants.

The opening notes of the Elephant Listening Project sounded in May 1984 with Asian elephants, not the forest elephants that would later dominate the group's research. Biologist Katy Payne sat in the elephant barn at the Washington Park Zoo in Portland, Oregon. For the last fifteen years, she and her husband, Roger, had been listening to humpback whales. Their exciting research on one of the largest

Although African forest elephants are related to African savanna elephants and Asian elephants, their DNA identifies them as a distinct species. Forest elephants are smaller than their savanna cousins, and their tusks are thinner.

marine mammals piqued Katy's curiosity about the sounds of elephants, the largest land mammals. As she listened in the zoo, sometimes the air around her throbbed and shuddered, a bit like distant thunder.

At the end of her visit, Katy boarded a plane for home. She closed her eyes and reflected on her time with the elephants. The throbbing of the airplane reminded her of the shuddering in the barn. Then came a memory of her thirteen-year-old self drawing breath to sing in a choir at Sage Chapel in Ithaca, New York. A grand pipe organ accompanied the singers. As the organist played, the air shuddered and throbbed. "The bass notes descended in a scale," Katy recalls. "The deeper they went, the slower the shuddering became. The pitch grew indistinct and muffled yet the shuddering grew stronger. I felt what I could not hear."

Were the elephants communicating with sounds too low for humans to hear? These sounds, known as infrasound, are normally associated with Earth-sized events, such as

Katy and Roger studied whales in Argentina for fifteen years. During that time, they learned that whales compose and sing complex songs.

avalanches, earthquakes, thunder, volcanoes, and severe storms. Katy knew that the largest whales used infrasound to communicate over long distances. Do elephants use it too? The scientist in Katy wanted to find out.

When Katy felt a throbbing in the air, she often saw a vibration in the center of an elephant's forehead.

SILENT THUNDER

FOUR MONTHS AFTER KATY'S FIRST VISIT TO THE WASHINGTON PARK ZOO, she returned with two colleagues, a borrowed tape recorder, high-tech microphones, and high hopes. They recorded forty-five hours of sound from eleven Asian elephants over seventeen days and two nights. As their tape recorder collected sounds, Katy and her team made detailed notes about the elephants' behavior. A baby named Sunshine trumpeted after spurting gallons of water on the floor with her trunk. Pet, an adult female, snorted as she corralled the last bits of hay on the floor. Tunga, a bull elephant, rumbled and growled as he paced his yard, frustrated at being separated from the other elephants at mating time. Sometimes—but not always—the research team felt a throbbing in the air.

Back home in Ithaca, Katy spoke with her longtime friend Carl Hopkins, a biology professor at Cornell University with a particular interest in animal communication. They had a hunch that elephants might communicate using infrasound. Katy thumbed through her notes for one of the times she'd felt a throbbing in the air and selected the matching audio tape. At the time, Rosy, the herd's matriarch, and Tunga had been standing on opposite sides of a wall. "If the wall had been removed, they would have been face-to-face," Katy says.

Wooooooooo! Rosy blew out through her trunk. *Slap-slap.* She flapped her ears against her neck. Carl rewound the tape and adjusted the settings on the recorder to make the tape play ten times faster. The faster speed raised the pitch by three octaves. Suddenly Carl and Katy could hear calls previously too low for their ears—calls in two distinct voices, one high and one low. Rosy and Tunga were carrying on a conversation below the level of human hearing! "A surprise discovery!" Katy says.

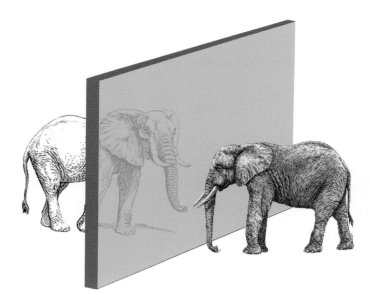

Rosy and Tunga chatted with each other from opposite sides of the wall.

Katy's close encounter with two Asian elephants in India in the late 1980s. "They were sweeping their trunks back and forth to each other in front of me," says Katy. She knew they were speaking with infrasound because she could feel the air throbbing.

For the first time ever, a research team had proven that Asian elephant calls contain infrasound. Could this be a clue to understanding how elephants communicate? Scientists already knew that low-pitched sounds travel farther than high sounds. So it's possible that infrasound might be used in long-distance communication—an amazing new twist in the study of elephant behavior.

Katy then wondered if African elephants also use infrasound. Biologists who study them had always marveled that elephant families separated by miles seem to stay in touch with one another. Perhaps scattered families of elephants use infrasound to coordinate where and when to meet. And maybe infrasound helps males and females, who live separately, find each other for mating.

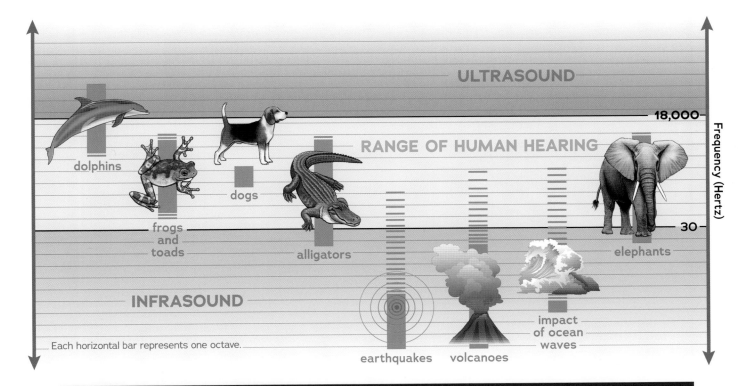

ULTRASOUND

18,000

RANGE OF HUMAN HEARING

dolphins

dogs

frogs
and
toads

alligators

earthquakes   volcanoes

impact
of ocean
waves

elephants

30

Frequency (Hertz)

INFRASOUND

Each horizontal bar represents one octave.

Some sounds in nature occur at frequencies outside of the typical range of human hearing. Sounds at frequencies too high for humans to hear are known as ultrasound. Elephants, volcanoes, and earthquakes can make sounds that are too low for humans to hear, called infrasound. The green bars on this graph show the range of frequencies for some common sounds in the natural world.

The search for answers led Katy on a five-year trek through Africa. Between 1986 and 1992, she visited the grassy plains of Kenya, the salt flats of Namibia, and the shrublands of Zimbabwe. She partnered with savanna elephant researchers who had studied the complex needs and family structure of these intelligent animals. The researchers had gathered strong evidence that elephants play, compete, celebrate, and grieve by observing behavior patterns and eavesdropping on conversations. They watched bull elephants possessively guard females from competing males. They watched seemingly joyful reunions full of rumbles and ear flapping. And they watched a procession of elephants roar and touch a dead family member. Through it all, Katy recorded the sounds they used to communicate.

Female savanna elephants and their young travel in large groups. Bulls (*below*) travel alone. When bulls meet, they often fight to protect their chosen mate or to declare their territory.

Elephants use trumpets, roars, rumbles, or a combination of these sounds to send messages. "The rumbles are the key to our story," Katy says, "for although elephants can hear them well, human beings cannot. Many are below our range of hearing."

Using acoustic recordings, Katy and her colleagues discovered that infrasound is part of a remarkable long-distance communication system in savanna elephants. It can travel across the grassy savanna and the dry plains nearly 2.5 miles (4 km). The rumbles function as social media to say hello, find a mate, and make plans—findings that formed the basis for later research by other scientists.

Katy suspected listening was the key to not only understanding these vocal animals but also to saving them. She needed to study all of their calls, not just the lowest notes, which meant expanding her studies beyond infrasound. Elephant researcher Andrea Turkalo offered to help her accomplish this goal.

Before the invention of digital technology, Katy recorded elephant sounds using reel-to-reel tape, like this 1988 device. A large battery (*right*) powered the recorder.

Andrea lived in the forest of Dzanga-Ndoki National Park in the Central African Republic. When she and Katy spoke in 1999, she'd been observing and recording forest elephants' behavior in an isolated clearing for nearly ten years. Her treasure trove of information about a different elephant species intrigued Katy.

At a meeting at Cornell University, Katy, Andrea, and scientists from Cornell's Bioacoustics Research Program agreed sound might help them better understand forest elephant habits. "We could find out who's there, who's troubled, who's thriving, how big the populations are, how they're using the day and night, and how they're using the landscape," Katy says. They had their eyes—and ears—on protecting the animals responsible for the health of the forest.

And so, fifteen years after Katy's team first discovered infrasonic calls in Asian elephants at an Oregon zoo, the Elephant Listening Project was established to study the calls of forest elephants. With Katy as its soft-spoken leader, the group decided to move beyond infrasound and focus on three questions that blazed a new trail in the field of elephant communication research: Could acoustic eavesdropping uncover more about forest elephants' habits? Could it help protect them? And could the combination of sound and behavior help scientists decode what elephants are saying to one another?

Katy packed her gear to visit Andrea in the forest.

Andrea (*left*) and Katy formed a unique partnership to find out more about forest elephant communication.

SEEING SOUND

Every call an elephant makes begins in its larynx, a tube-shaped organ that houses the vocal folds. Like the vocal folds in your larynx, puffs of air escape as the folds open and close, creating multiple vibrations.

Scientists can see these vibrations on a graph called a spectrogram. A rumble on a spectrogram looks like a stack of pancakes. The bottom "pancake" in the stack is the slowest vibration, or the fundamental frequency. It is sometimes too low for us to hear, or infrasonic. Even when Katy couldn't hear the first part of the rumble in the field, the spectrogram showed her it existed.

The other "pancakes" on the stack are the faster vibrations, or harmonics. Harmonics provide a layered richness to sound, much like instruments playing different parts in a band. The harmonics of an elephant rumble usually fall within our range of hearing.

The yellow or orange areas on the spectrogram show louder, stronger sounds with lots of energy behind them.

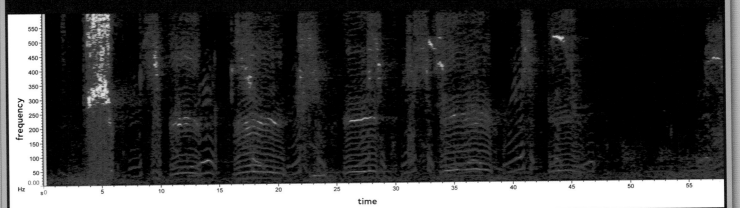

This spectrogram shows sixty seconds of elephant sounds. It opens with a roar (*the yellow-and-red column of noise on the left*), followed by several rumbles (*stacks of pancakes*).

Andrea's camp is located in the heart of the densely packed forest of trees in the Dzanga-Ndoki National Park.

WORKING IN HARMONY

KATY RECRUITED TWO RESEARCH ASSISTANTS, MYA THOMPSON AND MELISSA GROO, for her trip to central Africa. Together they designed detailed experiments and anticipated the physical challenges of the forest. Inside, they bubbled with excitement to see forest elephants in the wild.

The team paid two visits to Andrea in the equatorial forest—once during the wet season between May and July 2000, and again during the dry season between January and March 2002. Flying above the dense canopy for the first time, Katy looked down into the forest. "The Central African Republic forest is the second largest forest on Earth," she says. Hundreds of different kinds of trees form a barrier between sky and ground, hiding the forest elephants below. On Katy's earlier visit to Africa to study savanna elephants in Namibia, Zimbabwe, and Kenya, the wide-open plains allowed her to watch them from the air or from vehicles.

Katy knew these options wouldn't work for forest elephants. She had to travel deep into the forest to hear them.

After the researchers' teeth-rattling ride on bumpy roads, Andrea welcomed them to her compound near the Sangha, a "great, green, greasy river that flows into the Congo [River]," as Katy describes it. The compound was surprisingly comfortable. It included three one-room huts (one for Andrea and two for visitors), a hut for supplies, two bathing stalls, and a little farther away, an outhouse. In the center of these buildings stood an open-air structure with a thatched roof that served as a dining room and general meeting place. Solar panels provided enough electricity to power Andrea's computers and charge her camera batteries.

The compound seemed part of the wild landscape thanks to Andrea's careful planning and the help of local Bayaka people.

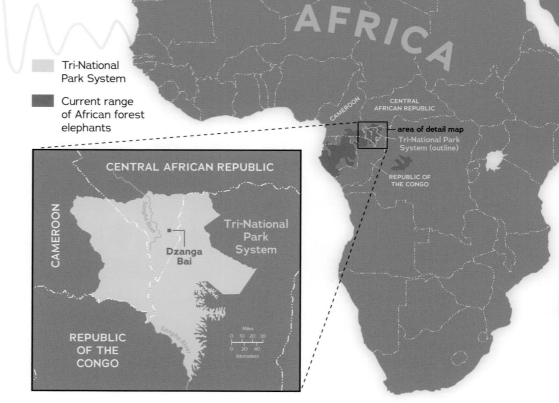

The Bayaka, known for their appreciation of nature, worked hand-in-hand with Andrea as camp staff, porters, trackers, and research assistants to help her protect the voices of the forest. Sesélé, who worked with Andrea the longest, said, "We Bayaka know the forest better than anyone. The forest is our original home. For many years we have kept Andrea safe among the elephants. That is the best a tracker can do."

As Katy's research team settled in for the night, the sounds of unseen animals crashing through the forest reminded them they weren't in Ithaca anymore. They crawled into bed under a canopy of mosquito netting and listened to a buzzy medley of crickets and cicadas accompanied by elephant trumpet blasts, percussive roars, and rumbling basses from a forest orchestra. The music reminded them they had come to listen.

The next afternoon, the group started the 1.2-mile (2 km) trek to the *bai*, the Bayaka word for forest clearing. The researchers carried cameras, tripods, notebooks, and acoustic recording units powered by large, heavy batteries. Katy, Mya, Melissa, Andrea, and the Bayaka assistants marched single file down a trail carved through the undergrowth by the feet of hundreds of elephants.

"We were surrounded by trees," Katy says. "Some of them very, very large, full of creatures I didn't know, full of birdsongs I wasn't familiar with, and so densely packed against each other you didn't see an animal until you were practically

The team crossed this swampy river twice a day—once to get to the *bai*, and once to return to Andrea's camp.

Sesélé was Andrea's head tracker during much of her time at Dzanga Bai.

on top of it." Dwarf crocodiles peered at them. *Ping, ping, ping* sang hundreds of frogs, like the twang of taut rubber bands being plucked. The researchers waded through ankle-deep mud past hundreds of butterflies sipping salt from patches of dirt where elephants had urinated.

Off the path, the forest seemed impenetrable: thorny, swampy, and impossible to navigate without a sharp machete and a strong arm to swing it. "It's a place where you really had to listen," Katy says. "Survival depended on it."

Before Dzanga Bai came into view, the team heard the screams and rumbles of elephants. The path led them to a thatched-roofed platform called a mirador. Like a proud matriarch showing off her family, Andrea led her guests up the steps for their first look at the elephants. "The clearing is a window into the forest," she says.

Dozens of elephants in small family groups dug narrow pits to reach the salty, mineral-rich water belowground. They sloshed

Andrea (*left*), Zou (*center*), and Nyele observe elephants from the mirador.

through a shallow stream that wandered through the rectangular-shaped *bai*, sometimes disturbing forest buffalo and small antelopes called sitatunga wallowing in the mud. Giddy baby elephants galloped through the water, scattering a kaleidoscope of butterflies. Snowy-white egrets shadowed the elephants to eat the bugs that hovered by the thousands around the great beasts. Two juvenile males practiced jousting at the far end of the *bai* while African grey parrots screeched and whistled overhead. And across from the mirador, a big male elephant lumbered into the clearing, perhaps in search of a mate. "The forest is truly the most inhabited place I've ever lived," Melissa says. "Every inch is taken up by some creature." And virtually all of them are dependent on forest elephants for survival.

At Dzanga Bai, elephants share the clearing with many different creatures, including bongos. Bongos are the largest antelopes in central Africa.

"Elephants are the architects of the forest," Andrea says. "They range wide. They eat a lot of fruit. And they defecate the seeds out all over the forest. A lot of these fruit trees wouldn't be around without elephants." When Andrea sifted through a pile of elephant dung, she found seeds from at least eight different tree species. Some scientists estimate that elephants distribute seeds for up to one-third of the trees in Africa's rain forests.

Andrea's data is vital to understanding how to preserve this keystone species. She has catalogued more than four thousand elephants that have visited the *bai* at one time or another. Each elephant has its own index card on which Andrea has noted the sex, specific ear tears or holes, the shape of the tail and tusks, eye color, the estimated age, the dates when they were seen, and their assigned name. Matriarchs have a Roman numeral I after their names, such as Kate I. Kate's children are labeled Kate II, Kate III, and so on, even if the calf is male. Andrea also jots down which elephants walk into the *bai* together and who spends time together.

This system helps her track elephant families. Without these detailed observations, the Elephant Listening Project's recorders would have captured random elephant sounds whose stories would remain a mystery. "We were interested in how sound and behavior went together," Katy says, and how that information could be applied to monitoring the well-being of elephants they couldn't see in other parts of the forest.

As Katy and her team stood on the mirador and admired the elephants' handiwork, they discussed where to put their recording devices for their experiments. They would soon discover the forest didn't always cooperate.

Hamilcar
A0? medium body stocky

30 Nov. 1992

Tusks: thick, curve inward. right higher than left 50 + 45ᶜᵐ r > l

Lobes: below

Tail: Long hair

An example of one of Andrea's index cards. Hamilcar is an adult male. His right tusk is longer than his left. What else does Andrea know about him?

ELEPHANT DICTIONARY: HELLO

On a peaceful day at the *bai*, two forest elephants named Kate I and Tess II met just below the mirador. Amid the cheeps of birds and the croaks of frogs, they greeted each other with high-energy rumbles that seemed to communicate more than a simple hello. Their two distinct voices were heard—one higher than the other. Sometimes they rumbled separately, and sometimes they rumbled together, as if they were saying, "Oh, I haven't seen you for so long! How have you been?" Ear flapping, tail waving, trunk curling, and swaying accompanied the calls. Did these gestures emphasize their excitement?

"Greetings can vary between individual elephants," Andrea says. "Some walk by and flap their ears and some are very vocal. Perhaps Kate and Tess had been separated for a long time and . . . there's a lot of enthusiasm and joy in finding each other again." The Elephant Listening Project is just beginning to figure out what it all might mean.

When Kate and Tess finished their conversation, they grazed together in comfortable silence, seemingly happy to be together again. Scan the QR code below to see a video of this interaction between Katie I and Tess II.

http://qrs.lernerbooks.com/atfz

Three elephants say hello.

23

Elephants dig pits to reach underground minerals essential to their diet.

VERSE 3

MUSICIANS OF THE FOREST

AFTER THEIR INITIAL INTRODUCTION TO THE WONDERS OF DZANGA BAI, Katy, Mya, and Melissa settled down to the business of science. Digital recorders had to be positioned, and elephants had to be observed and counted.

The team planned to record elephant sounds using six acoustic recording units around the *bai*. Once the units were activated, they would provide three months of continuous recording. Each unit included a microphone to collect the forest sounds and a computer circuit board to save the sounds to a hard drive much like the one in a laptop. Packing foam inside a plastic lunch box cushioned the device against casual bumps from passing elephants or curious monkeys.

The team scouted for good places around the *bai* to put the recording devices that would lead to maximum sound coverage.

As with most tasks in the forest, placing the units required courage and agility.

Elephants rule the forest, so before the team approached the desired spot for each recording unit, they waited for elephants to leave the area. "The elephants are under increasing poaching pressure and their contagious fear seems to be building," Mya says. Occasionally an elephant family surprised the team and they scampered up nearby trees to safety—trees that were sometimes full of biting ants.

At first, the team set up the recorders on the ground, but a curious elephant tusked one of the lunch boxes. "It was a real bummer when we found that case on the ground all torn apart but also a good reminder about who was in charge!" Mya says. The scientists felt pressure to work quickly with the hope their data would improve the elephants' long-term survival.

Plan B sent the team up the trees—without being chased this time. Engineer Eric Spaulding (who joined Katy's team in 2002) recruited a couple of Andrea's Bayaka assistants to

help. Rain forest trees do not usually have low-hanging limbs for climbing. The trunks shoot 130 feet (40 m) into the air and are ramrod straight, but the Bayaka men shinnied up them as easily as they might climb stairs.

Before an elephant tusked one of the recording devices, Katy's team hid them on the ground.

Mya (*left front*) and Melissa (*right*) work on the mirador with Bayaka assistants Koto (*left*) and Melebu (*center*).

They tossed a rope over the nearest limb. Eric tied one end of the rope to the recording unit and pulled on the other end to haul it into the air. The assistants then fastened the unit to a sturdy branch well above the elephants' reach.

While the recording units "listened" day and night, Katy and her team tested whether the number of elephant calls could help them estimate the number of elephants in the area.

The researchers gazed through long-range scopes to count elephants on the *bai* every half hour. They kept track of these counts in a field notebook to refer back to when they listened to the sound recordings at home in the lab.

They also gathered behavioral information to help decode what the elephants said to one another. Then they plotted each elephant's location on a map of the *bai*. When they listened to the recordings in the lab later, they hoped the map would help them figure out who made the call. Andrea also took attendance as the day grew later (and hotter) and more elephants came to the *bai*. She identified each elephant using her index cards to help Katy's team learn how the elephants were related. Understanding the elephants' family structure might help the team assign meanings to the calls. Lastly, Melissa, Mya, and the Bayaka assistants filmed activity on the *bai*. The video and sound recordings combined would help the researchers match behaviors with sounds and sort them into categories such as greetings, protest calls, alarm calls, rumbles to find a mate, and an infant calling its mother.

For instance, in one video clip the dominant Gonya family foraged at one end of the *bai*, while the Penelope family wandered the *bai*'s crisscrossing trails. A Penelope family infant played in the water, moving farther and farther from her family.

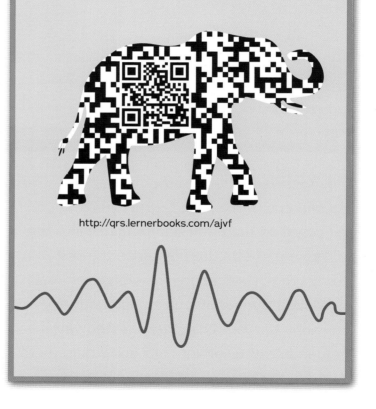

LISTEN UP!

The Elephant Listening Project must pick out elephant sounds from the rest of the forest symphony. Practice your listening skills with these forest sounds.

http://qrs.lernerbooks.com/ajvf

The Gonya family was at the center of a drama that played out on the *bai* when Katy and her team visited.

The Penelope family rushes across the *bai* to save their infant.

All of a sudden, the infant's terrified scream shattered the peace. The Gonya matriarch was dunking the Penelope infant in a puddle. The Gonyas surrounded the infant, their deep rumblings possibly sending out a warning. The infant screamed again, and its mother, Penelope II, charged toward the Gonyas followed by the infant's older sibling, grandmother, and a couple of aunts.

The Gonyas strolled away, clearly uninterested in a fight, while Penelope relatives trumpeted and rumbled. Did they say good riddance? Thank you? Was Mama Gonya being mean, or did she want the calf to call its mother? According to Katy, one possible guess might be, "The Gonyas knew the calf wasn't one of them and they were getting rid of it." As quickly as the drama started, it stopped.

Katy hoped that watching this story unfold on video and hearing it on the recordings would help her team identify infant distress calls in the future, even when a calf is hidden deep in the forest. "The better we get at interpreting elephants' calls and calling patterns, the closer we'll come to valid interpretation of recordings without matching observations," Katy says. A better understanding of elephant communication means that park managers and conservationists can make more informed decisions about how to give elephants the space they need to thrive.

At the end of their two field seasons, Katy and her team packed up their recording units, said goodbye to Andrea, and returned

Mya listens to recorded Dzanga Bai sounds.

to Ithaca. They turned their attention to the next phase of their project: sifting through hours of data to look for patterns in elephant calling behavior.

ELEPHANT DICTIONARY: GOODBYE

Morna I led her sick calf, Morna IV, to the *bai*. Eventually the calf collapsed next to a flowing stream and died.

Over the next few days, many elephants approached Morna IV's little corpse, smelling, touching, and rumbling. They stood close, as if guarding her body. But two in particular struck Katy and Andrea. Oria I and her son tried to roll Morna IV over using their trunks. Ears flapping, they circled the body and nudged her with their feet. They rumbled and trumpeted several times. Then the young male let loose a roar seemingly filled with anguish. His grief echoed across the *bai*.

"One hundred twenty-seven elephants walked along that path that day and . . . the next day," Katy says. "And about a quarter of them tried to move the body. Many of them made distress calls." Based on her studies of elephant communication, Katy assumed infrasound was helping the elephants spread the word.

Throughout the procession, Morna I remained near her baby. Was she grieving? From our perspective as humans, it seems so. "We were most interested in events that contained behaviors we could understand or empathize with," Katy says. Watch the elephants mourn for Morna IV by scanning the QR code.

Equinox says goodbye to Morna's calf.

http://qrs.lernerbooks.com/atg1

Forest elephant families work together to look after young calves. What would Andrea's ID card look like for this mother and calf?

VERSE 4

FOREST DYNAMICS

WHEN KATY, MYA, AND MELISSA RETURNED FROM DZANGA BAI, they opened their moldy-smelling recording units and started the long process of analyzing data. The six units contained more than twenty thousand precious hours of sound they hoped would help answer the Elephant Listening Project's three main questions: Could acoustic eavesdropping uncover more about forest elephants' habits? Could it help protect them? And could the combination of sound and behavior help scientists decode what elephants are saying to one another?

First, the team had to manage the mountain of data. Fortunately, technology came to their rescue in the form of a computer program. Rather than manually finding the sound recordings from all six units for any one date, the program automatically organized them. To listen to elephant sounds from January 15, 2002, for instance, one click of the mouse displayed all six files on Katy's computer screen for easy listening.

Once the data files were organized, the trio tracked the number of elephant calls with another computer program that created a spectrogram—a visual picture of forest sounds. The distinctive stacked structure of elephant rumbles allowed the team to see and count the sounds. Simple, right? Yes, but the sheer amount of data overwhelmed the tiny Elephant Listening Project staff. Mya and Melissa set weekly goals to get through it all. "I remember starting to see elephant rumble spectrograms in my dreams and in the shapes of clouds," Mya says.

Katy, Mya, and Melissa returned to their original research question. Could they estimate the number of elephants in a group by counting elephant calls? The answer was tricky because some days elephants don't say anything. Other days they talk a lot. The team compared the spectrogram call counts with the elephant counts from their field notebooks over many days and discovered more elephants generate more calls. Their findings opened the door to a reliable new way for researchers to

The huge surface area of an elephant's ears allow it to capture a variety of sounds, including infrasound. The blood vessels near the surface of the skin also help the elephant cool off.

count elephants invisible in the dense forest. Traditionally, scientists walk along elephant trails counting dung piles to estimate the number of elephants in an area, but they're limited by the amount of forest one person can cover on foot. Technology came to the rescue again. Each acoustic recording device covers nearly 1.3 square miles (3.2 sq. km) of forest, which allows scientists to listen to larger swaths, a time-saving idea in the race to protect elephants. If scientists know where elephants spend time, they can determine whether conservation efforts are working.

After Katy, Mya, and Melissa made their important discovery, the Elephant Listening Project's story took a few unexpected turns. Between 2004 and 2006, several staff changes occurred. Mya left to pursue a PhD inspired by her work in Dzanga Bai. Melissa changed careers and became a professional wildlife photographer. And Liz Rowland, who worked in another department at Cornell University, came on the scene after hearing one of Katy's on-campus talks. Liz became keeper of the data.

Liz listens to elephant rumbles. Her computer software helps her identify and count them.

She analyzed Dzanga Bai sound files and helped Katy prepare for the flood of presentations and interviews that her research generated.

Katy officially retired from the Elephant Listening Project at the age of sixty-nine. Although she still travels and speaks on behalf of elephants, she no longer manages the project's day-to-day work. Her director's baton passed to Peter Wrege (rhymes with Greg), a behavioral ecologist. "Peter is the voice of the future," Katy says.

When Peter came on board in 2007, he and Liz reviewed the Elephant Listening Project's three defining questions: Could scientific eavesdropping help them learn more about forest elephants? Could it help protect them? And could the combination of sound and behavior help scientists decode what elephants are saying to one another?

In a sobering reality check, Peter initially decided to set aside the question of what elephants are saying to focus on protecting them. "There are so many things working against the forest's long-term survival," he says.

Poaching, logging, mining, and an increasing human population take resources from the forest without putting anything back. "Figuring out the language of elephants is interesting from an academic perspective," Peter says. "But if we lose the elephants altogether, there's no point in figuring out their language. I need to be putting my effort into keeping them alive."

According to Andrea, forest elephants spend only 2 percent of their time in clearings—a tiny portion of their lives. Peter could use Katy's findings that showed larger numbers of elephants generate more calls to find out what parts of the forest were important to them. If he knew where elephants spent time, he could alert park managers to protect those places.

Peter expanded the Elephant Listening Project's eavesdropping beyond the Central African Republic. He assembled teams of local assistants and climbed dozens of trees to mount recording units in Gabon, Cameroon, and the Republic of the Congo. Unlike Katy and Andrea, Peter did not observe the elephants from a platform. He simply recorded their calls within the dense forest.

Logging activities change the landscape of the forest, not only removing habitat but also altering the way that elephants and other forest creatures behave.

Back in Ithaca, Liz recruited enthusiastic Cornell student volunteers to listen to and analyze the data Peter collected. Liz trained students to recognize elephant rumbles, trumpets, roars, and screams from the symphony of other forest sounds on the recordings. Peter then used the data to help countries make informed conservation decisions about a keystone species critical to the forest's survival.

With their new plan in place, Peter and Liz determined listening to elephants is making a difference.

In Gabon, one company paid the government for the right to explore for oil in a national park. Heavy trucks rumbled on new roads carved out of dense forest. Human voices intruded on the music of the forest. Dynamite blasted holes in the earth. Park managers guessed that the elephants would get scared and leave the area. Two groups of scientists wondered if the park managers were right. One group counted dung piles. Peter and his team put recording units in trees. After several months, they compared results.

Peter prepares to haul a recording unit into a tree. Field scientists often have to solve problems on the spot. Peter comes prepared with a variety of tools to work in the humid forest.

Both sets of data showed the elephants had not left the park as expected. From the dung counts alone, scientists might have assumed that because elephants stuck around, they were not affected by the unfamiliar noises. "But we showed there was an effect," Peter says. The recording devices picked up elephant rumbles, trumpets, and roars not during daylight hours but at night. "The elephants became nocturnal and hunkered down somewhere during the day," Peter says. Dung counts alone were not sufficient to see this change in the elephants' behavior.

Park managers allowed oil exploration to continue, but using Peter's sound data, they changed the rules to respect the elephants' new habits. "No vehicles or people were allowed on the roads after dark," Peter says. "When it got dark and the vehicles stopped moving, elephants emerged from their refuges to search for fruits, find mates, and connect with extended family to catch up on the news." Peter provided similar data to a logging company in another Gabonese park. The loggers also changed their practices to give the elephants space.

For nearly ten years, Peter and Liz (and their ever-changing family of student volunteers) worked together. They listened to elephants all over the central African rain forest, a two-person-plus rescue team dedicated to saving the mysterious forest elephant. Peter also visited the Elephant Listening Project's first voices—the elephants of Dzanga Bai—and reconnected with his love of animal behavior. His earlier decision to postpone the study of elephant language and the role of infrasound began to gnaw at him. Although infrasound had dominated Katy's early

Cornell student volunteers listen to and categorize elephant calls. According to Liz, training each volunteer takes about fifteen hours.

work with Asian and savanna elephants, it didn't define either hers or Peter's work with forest elephants. Peter decided to make a change. The Elephant Listening Project needed to dig deeper into the dynamics of forest elephant sounds, not just to find out where they spent time but also to explain their language and the role of infrasound.

Enter Daniela Hedwig, a German scientist fresh from her PhD studies on gorilla communication in the mountains bordering Africa's Rift Valley and the rain forests near Dzanga Bai. Peter hired her in 2016 to explore the complex world of elephant language, a mystery that could take years to unravel. She began with two questions: How do forest elephants use infrasound to communicate? And what do their roars and rumbles mean?

Daniela started her research on infrasound with sounds collected by Peter and Liz years earlier at a study site in Gabon. She measured how far the lowest sounds in an elephant rumble traveled. Under calm winds and periods of low noise, savanna elephants' infrasonic calls can travel as far as 2.5 miles (4 km) over the

Daniela Hedwig on the mirador on her first trip to Dzanga Bai.

hard, sandy soil. Forest elephants are probably capable of producing rumbles that travel as far under similar low noise and low wind conditions, but forest conditions are rarely ideal.

Daniela found that forest elephant infrasound traveled a little more than half a mile (1 km). "I was really surprised," she says, but after some thought, her results made sense to her. "The vegetation is so dense." The sound attenuates, or is absorbed by the huge amount of plant life in the forest. "This has some serious implications for how the elephants coordinate family groups, how they orchestrate reunions, and how they come together and exchange information," she says. Perhaps infrasound isn't as important to forest elephants. Maybe related family groups have an internal seasonal clock that tells them when to meet, and the information is passed down from mother to child. On the other hand, perhaps infrasound is a vital form of communication and forest elephants wait for quiet periods to send their messages over long distances. No one knows. Yet. But Daniela is eavesdropping on elephants for the answers.

Daniela picked up where Katy left off, looking at what specific elephant sounds might mean. "Within one rumble, there's the potential for an awful lot of information to be encoded," Liz says. "For instance, this is who I am. Or I'm feeling this way. Or there's a good deal on bananas two blocks down."

As a first step, Daniela wants to know what an elephant roar means. Sometimes an infant roars when it becomes separated from its mother. Other times two adults roar as they compete for the same waterhole. "But sometimes they have a rumble attached— either before the roar, or after it, or both," Daniela says. She studies the elephants' behavior using a database of Dzanga Bai videos from the 2000 and 2002 field seasons. Melissa's notes about each video identify the elephants and describe the behavior in the clip. Daniela wants to know if the behavior for a roar used alone differs from the behavior for a roar-rumble combination. If the behaviors are indeed different, Daniela can guess at the meanings of those calls.

Katy's original vision for combining forest elephant sounds with behaviors has been compared to a dictionary of sorts. To develop the dictionary, Daniela must first learn the language. When she's fluent enough, the sounds that Peter recorded can be analyzed again. Perhaps the Elephant Listening Project will begin to understand elephant conversations. And understanding could lead to new ideas in the fight to save this keystone species.

A three-way battle for the same pit. Elephants rumble and roar when they compete for resources.

ELEPHANT DICTIONARY: HAPPY BIRTHDAY

On the afternoon of February 15, 2012, Equinox I gave birth to her sixth calf. Officially, he's Equinox VII, but Andrea nicknamed him Valentine. A birth is big news in the elephant world. Other females clambered to smell and touch Equinox I and Valentine. As the herd jockeyed for position around the calf, Andrea and Peter feared Valentine's adoring fans would accidentally step on him! Screams, roars, rumbles, and ear flapping punctuated their excitement—and, Andrea suspected, a lot of infrasound to share the news. "In all the commotion, it's a wonder the offspring even survives," Andrea says.

Andrea had seen a birth only one other time from her mirador. "Usually females prefer not to give birth in the *bai* because of the interference of other individuals," she says. And after the hard day Equinox I had, Andrea believes she won't ever do it again! See the birthing celebration by scanning the QR code below.

http://qrs.lernerbooks.com/atg3

Valentine's admirers look on as he tries to stand for the first time.

Tusks are actually teeth that never stop growing during an elephant's life. Large tusks are becoming rare because of ivory poaching.

CONSERVATION CHORUS

ELEPHANTS ARE RESPONSIBLE FOR THE BLASTS, ROARS, RUMBLES, SCREAMS, AND GRUNTS of the forest symphony. And Katy, currently in her eighties, has dedicated much of her life to appreciating their sounds. "I see my responsibility as being to listen," she says, because this keystone species reminds us that we share the planet with billions of other living things. Each choice we make affects the forest symphony—the elephants and the plant and animal life they support.

Katy's listening studies opened a window on the mysterious habits of forest elephants that would otherwise have remained invisible in the dense landscape. By understanding where they go and how they use the forest, scientists can make informed conservation decisions to save a species that benefits nearly all other forest life. And Katy's trailblazing partnership with Andrea established a catalogue of sounds that go along with the behaviors for alarm calls, mating, greeting, birth, and death.

So, what does the future hold for the Elephant Listening Project?

Daniela follows Katy's example to decode elephant conversations. After analyzing the specific meanings of rumble-roar combinations, she will focus on the structure of the rumbles. Does a long rumble mean something different than a short one? Is an infrasonic rumble different from an audible one? Do the rumbles differ among different groups of elephants? Most of us assume that elephants speak only

A good example of alarm behavior in an adult female. She spreads her ears wide to catch the slightest sounds, and her feet are ready to run.

one version of Elephant. But suppose there are different dialects of Elephant just as there are different dialects of English and Spanish? "We have data from Dzanga, from various places in Gabon, from the Republic of the Congo, in clearings and within the forest," Daniela says. "It would be really great to see if there are differences in their vocal behavior."

Andrea's thirty years of forest elephant observations give scientists a rare look at this secretive species when they come to the *bai*. But it's not enough. "In a way, it's like what we would know about humans if we only observed them in a classroom and never anywhere else," Peter says. Listening draws back the curtain of dense forest foliage to help scientists figure out what elephants do with the rest of their time. As Peter demonstrated, this information guides conservation decisions that help elephants coexist with loggers, miners, and oil explorers.

Although these industries provide valuable jobs for local people, Andrea worries about habitat loss. Between 2002 and 2011, forest elephants lost one-third of their home range to human activity. "One hundred years ago, people were surrounded by elephants. Now elephants are surrounded by people," Andrea says. "Once those natural resources are removed, and this includes the wildlife, the people will be poorer than they are now."

The region's true wealth lies in the rain forest. The Bayaka people can read animal tracks, identify thousands of plants to eat or use as medicines, find honey from the flight path of a single bee, and know the flowering and fruiting cycles of plants. "The forest belongs to the Bayaka the way it belongs to the elephants," Sesélé says.

The forest also removes large amounts of carbon dioxide released by cars, trucks, airplanes, and factories that burn coal, oil, and gasoline. Plants on land and in the ocean absorb some of this carbon dioxide. But as Andrea says, forest habitat has already been destroyed. The remaining plants cannot keep up to bring Earth back into balance. Greenhouse gases such as carbon dioxide contribute to climate change.

A logging road opens up the forest to more than just loggers.

Imagine if the second-largest forest on the planet disappeared. Everything that lives in the forest—including elephants—could also disappear. "The Bayaka get it," Andrea says. "We have to conserve natural resources to have something for the future."

Andrea also worries about the political climate of the forest nations. In 2013, rebels took over the government of the Central African Republic. Chaos followed. Andrea fled with only a change of clothes and six hard drives of data. She could not return for a year and a half. During that time, at least twenty-six Dzanga Bai elephants—mostly females and their calves—were massacred for their ivory tusks.

Rebel armies often finance wars by poaching wildlife. "When an elephant is killed it is as if we have lost one of our family," Sesélé says. Political unrest and war devastates local people and wildlife.

Equally devastating are the new roads that industry slashes through the forest. These roads tempt poachers into wild places previously off-limits. Between 2002 and 2011, 62 percent of the world's forest elephants were killed for their tusks. Most of the tusks went to Asia and specifically China, which is the world's largest consumer of ivory. By 2014, China's demand for ivory drove up the price to $955 per pound (0.5 kg). A pair of male elephant tusks can weigh up to 250 pounds (113 kg). Fortunately for elephants, China closed its ivory trade at the end of 2017 and the price of ivory is falling.

But even with this glimmer of good news, Andrea estimates that forest elephants will take at least eighty years—an entire lifetime—to recover from poaching. Her studies from Dzanga Bai suggest that forest elephants have an extremely low birth rate, which

A soldier with the World Wildlife Fund's eco-guards shows two ivory tusks confiscated from poachers in the Central African Republic.

means the forest will suffer as forest elephant populations decrease.

In the meantime, Peter and Liz continue to listen to the music of the forest. "Since 2007, we've recorded six hundred thousand hours of sound from the Central African forest," Peter says. "Monkeys, frogs, crickets, insects, anything that makes noise." Including guns. Peter uses acoustic recordings to learn more about hunting patterns.

In a two-year study in Cameroon's Korup National Park, Peter discovered an increase in hunting activity that other survey methods failed to pick up. Hunting peaked at midnight when few anti-poaching units patrolled the park and on Tuesdays, Wednesdays, and

Thursdays—most likely to have meat and ivory to sell at the Saturday market. And more hunting occurred in the dry season, especially around Christmas and New Year's Day. If park managers redistribute their anti-poaching efforts using these findings, Peter can measure if they have any effect.

While the Elephant Listening Project listens to forest elephants, you can bet the elephants are listening to our trucks, explosions, drills, and gunshots. Their survival depends on it. Death by humans overshadows every other danger in their forest home. Peter showed that forest elephants change ancient meeting traditions because of oil exploration, logging, and presumably other activity in the forest.

The Elephant Listening Project and Andrea have become the world's leading experts on forest elephants. But they have so much more to learn. "It's frightening," Peter says. "We're being forced by poaching into making decisions and trying to do what we can, but we don't really have all the cards to know what's right." In his effort to find out more about what forest elephants do in the forest, Peter has stepped up his listening. He trained two Congolese assistants to install fifty recording devices in a grid-like array in the forest of the Republic of the Congo. It took them nearly two months! While the recorders "listen" for two years to more than 580 square miles (1,500 sq. km), Peter hopes to hear a more complete picture of the elephants' habits, their migration patterns, and what parts of the forest are important to them.

Peter trains his assistant, Clement, to program the recording devices before installing them in trees. Peter hopes that local people will continue to gather elephant sounds with recorders leased from the Elephant Listening Project.

In the future, Peter hopes to collect elephant sounds more easily. He imagines one day using drones to drop acoustic recorders hanging from parachutes into the forest instead of trekking along narrow trails with heavy equipment. The parachute might have solar panels to power the device. If Peter gets his wish, the recording unit itself will sift out the elephant calls and send small sound clips to Ithaca via satellite, rather than forcing him and his assistants to climb trees to retrieve the stored sounds. "I don't know how to do any of that," Peter says. So, he waits . . .

Perhaps he waits for someone like you with the right technical know-how to design an easier way to study forest elephants. Or perhaps you could join the conservation chorus by sharing the Elephant Listening Project's story with your family and friends. Maybe learning more about forest elephants inspired you to help save endangered species near your home and in other parts of the world.

"I think that children's voices and what children care about make a huge difference in this world," Katy says. "And they must be given a bigger voice. Schools are getting better at it, but we have to go beyond schools."

Perhaps your role will take you to the field as a scientist like Katy, Andrea, and Peter. Perhaps you will learn the building blocks of language to help Daniela understand these giants of the forest. Or perhaps you will listen to and analyze data like Liz.

"Elephants gave me a purpose," Andrea says. "It was like a gift being given to me." Perhaps a similar opportunity will change your life.

Whatever path you take, remember that listening is the key. What would it be like to hear with an elephant's ears? Listening connects us to the music in our environment and shows us how our habits affect the world around us. The more you listen to wildlife, the more your mind opens up to new ideas about why the world is a place worth saving. "If we learn to listen as well as elephants do, it is possible that listening will keep the world safe," Katy says.

ELEPHANT DICTIONARY: I'M THE BOSS

One dry January day, a bull elephant named Habib arrived at Dzanga Bai in musth, a condition that made him exceptionally aggressive, a little kooky, and ready to mate. He barreled through streams, sniffed adult females, chased birds, and made a spectacle of himself. His rumbles seemed to say he was king of the forest.

Moments later, an older and bigger musth bull announced his presence with a deep, ominous rumble. At fifty-plus years old, Eli demands respect from young studs who think they have breeding rights on the *bai*. But Habib wasn't about to give up his claim to the throne so easily.

They faced off at the far edge of the *bai*. Almost immediately they locked tusks and shoved. Adult females and their young flapped their ears, trumpeted, and ran to and fro to show their excitement. Near-constant rumbles echoed through the *bai*. "Most of the vocalizations are probably coming from the onlookers," Andrea says.

Habib and Eli kicked up clouds of dust as their powerful legs adjusted to maximize their pushing power. They tangled in and out of the undergrowth. Finally, Eli shoved Habib backward into a dead tree trunk. The trunk fell on Habib, who seemed to let out a groan of frustration. Eli prodded Habib from behind with his tusks until Habib ran away with a roar of defeat. Scan the QR code to see the standoff between Habib and Eli for yourself.

http://qrs.lernerbooks.com/atg4

Eli (*left*) and Habib (*right*) battle at the edge of Dzanga Bai.

MAKING A DIFFERENCE
TAEGEN YARDLEY

Middle schooler Taegen Yardley learned about the plight of elephants by watching a documentary called *Battle for the Elephants*. She decided to add her voice to the conservation chorus by organizing a march for elephant awareness in her Vermont hometown to coincide with the annual Global March for Elephants and Rhinos. The documentary also inspired her to make her own movies. Her first film won her an invitation to speak to wildlife conservation leaders from the US and several African countries.

Watch Taegen's movies to inspire your own ideas about elephant conservation.

"Kids Battling for a World with Elephants"
https://www.youtube.com/watch?v=nXq6gk2Tgd0

"#YoungVoicesforWildlife"
https://www.youtube.com/watch?v=oVTUUbr4NXQ

Taegen Yardley organized a Global March for Elephants in Vermont. She created ninety-six pairs of model elephant tusks to symbolize the ninety-six elephants killed each day by poachers.

SOURCE NOTES

5 Katharine Payne, *Elephants Calling*, (New York: Crown Publishers, 1992), 36.

7 Katy Payne, *Silent Thunder: In the Presence of Elephants* (New York: Simon & Schuster, 1998), 21.

10 Payne, *Silent Thunder*, 27.

10 Katy Payne, interview with the author, April 4, 2017.

10 Katy Payne, interview with the author, April 6, 2016.

13 Katy Payne, "Elephant Talk," *National Geographic* 176, no. 2 (August 1989): 266.

14 Krista Tippett, "Katy Payne: In the Presence of Elephants and Whales," August 13, 2015, *On Being*, produced by Chris Heagle, Maia Tarrell, and Maria Simbilay, podcast, MP3 audio, 12:34.

17 Payne, interview, April 4, 2017.

18 Katy Payne, "Letters from the Field: Katy Payne," *NPR*, October 31, 2002, https://www.npr.org/templates/story/story.php?storyId=3879218.

18 Sesélé, interview with Todd McGrain, dir. *Elephant Path/Njaia Njoku*, October–November 2014.

19–20 Payne, interview, April 4, 2017.

20 Payne, interview, April 4, 2017.

20 Andrea Turkalo, interview with the author, March 21, 2017.

21 Melissa Groo, "Letters from the Field: Melissa Groo," *NPR*, October 31, 2002, http://www.npr.org/templates/story/story.php?storyId=3879220.

21 Turkalo, interview, March 21, 2017.

22 Payne, interview, April 6, 2017.

23 Andrea Turkalo, interview with the author, April 26, 2017.

26 Mya Thompson, "Letters from the Field: Mya Thompson," *NPR*, October 31, 2002, https://www.npr.org/templates/story/story.php?storyId=3879216.

26 Mya Thompson, email message to the author, May 18, 2017.

29 Payne, interview, April 4, 2017.

30 Payne, "Letters from the Field."

31 Payne, interview, April 4, 2017.

31 Payne, interview, April 4, 2017.

34 Mya Thompson, email message to the author, July 24, 2017.

35 Payne, interview, April 4, 2017.

35 Peter Wrege, interview with the author, April 4, 2017.

36 Wrege, interview, April 4, 2017.

37 Wrege, interview, April 4, 2017.

38 Wrege, interview, April 4, 2017.

39 Daniela Hedwig, interview with the author, April 6, 2017.

39 Hedwig, interview, April 6, 2017.

40 Elizabeth Rowland, interview with the author, April 5, 2017.

40 Hedwig, interview, April 6, 2017.

41 Andrea Turkalo, interview with the author, April 6, 2017.

41 Turkalo, interview, April 6, 2017.

43 Tippett, "Katy Payne," 26:03.

44 Hedwig, interview, April 6, 2017

44 Peter Wrege, interview with the author, November 15, 2016.

45 Turkalo, interview, March 21, 2017.

45 Sesélé, interview with Todd McGrain.

45 Turkalo, interview, March 21, 2017.

46 Sesélé, interview with Todd McGrain.

46 Wrege, interview, April 4, 2017.

47 Wrege, interview, November 15, 2016.

48 Peter Wrege, interview with the author, April 6, 2017.

48 Katy Payne, interview with the author, November 14, 2016.

48 Turkalo, interview, April 26, 2017.

48 Payne, *Elephants Calling*, 36.

49 Andrea Turkalo, email message to the author, June 16, 2017.

GLOSSARY

acoustic: relating to sound or hearing

array: a series or arrangement, as in several acoustic recording units arranged around a forest clearing

attenuate: to reduce the energy behind a sound

bai: the Bayaka word for forest clearing

Bayaka: people of the central African rain forest who are excellent trackers and are known for their knowledge of the forest

behavior: the way animals act or react to one another and their environment

bull: a male elephant

conservation: the careful protection and preservation of the variety of plant and animal life

frequency: the rate of vibration of a sound wave—the faster the movement, the higher the pitch

fundamental frequency: the lowest frequency produced by the vibration of an elephant's vocal folds

harmonics: a series of overtones above the fundamental frequency exactly the same distance apart from one another on a spectrogram

infrasound: sound below the level of human hearing

ivory: the material of an elephant's tusks

keystone species: a species on which other species depend for survival in an ecosystem

larynx: a tube-shaped organ in the neck of air-breathing mammals that contains the vocal folds

matriarch: the female elephant who rules and protects her family group

mirador: an observation platform, from the Spanish word *mirar*, which means to look

musth: a bull elephant's condition where the urge to mate is very strong. During this time, a bull elephant is aggressive and territorial.

poaching: illegal hunting of wild animals for profit

spectrogram: a graph of acoustic data that shows a visual representation of sound

vocal folds: membranes of tissue in a mammal's throat that open and close when the animal makes sound

vocalizations: sounds produced by elephants or any other animal, such as whales and birds

SELECTED BIBLIOGRAPHY

Groo, Melissa. "Letters from the Field: Melissa Groo." *NPR*, October 31, 2002. http://www.npr.org/templates/story/story.php?storyId=3879220.

Payne, Katharine (retired director, Elephant Listening Project). Interview by the author, November 14, 2016, April 4 and 6, 2017.

Payne, Katharine B., Mya Thompson, and Laura Kramer. "Elephant Calling Patterns as Indicators of Group Size and Composition: The Basis for an Acoustic Monitoring System." *African Journal of Ecology* 41 (March 14, 2003): 99–107.

Rowland, Elizabeth D. (research assistant, Elephant Listening Project). Interview by the author, April 5, 2017.

Simon, Bob. "The Secret Language of Elephants." December 28, 2014. http://www.cbsnews.com/news/the-secret-language-of-elephants2/.

Turkalo, Andrea K. (biologist, Wildlife Conservation Society and Elephant Listening Project). Interview by the author, March 21 and 31, April 6 and 26, 2017.

Wrege, Peter H. (director, Elephant Listening Project). Interview by the author, November 15, 2016, April 4 and 6, 2017.

CODA: ON ELEPHANTS AND CONSERVATION

BOOKS

Buzzeo, Toni, and Holly Berry. *A Passion for Elephants: The Real Life Adventure of Field Scientist Cynthia Moss.* New York: Dial Books, 2015.
Cynthia Moss and Katy Payne worked together when Katy recorded infrasound in savanna elephants. Read this book to see how Cynthia became one of the foremost scientists to study the world's largest land animal.

Newman, Patricia, and Annie Crawley. *Zoo Scientists to the Rescue.* Minneapolis: Millbrook Press, 2018.
Zoos take care of animals and welcome visitors of all ages, but that's not all zoos do. Step behind the scenes at three zoos to meet scientists working to save orangutans, black-footed ferrets, and black rhinoceroses.

O'Connell, Caitlin, and Donna M. Jackson. *The Elephant Scientist.* Boston: Houghton Mifflin Harcourt, 2011.
Katy Payne recorded elephant vocalizations and infrasound with tree-mounted units in the forest, and Caitlyn O'Connell measured how savanna elephants communicate via ground vibrations on the savanna. Read about Caitlyn's experiments and her discoveries.

Roy, Katherine. *How to Be an Elephant.* New York: David Macauley Studio, 2017.
This beautifully illustrated nonfiction book describes how a newborn elephant grows into an adult with the help of its family.

Stanek, Linda, and Shennen Bersani. *Once Upon an Elephant.* Mount Pleasant, SC: Arbordale, 2016.
Elephants are superheroes of the savanna. They dig wells for thirsty animals. They eat small trees to keep the grasslands open. They find precious salt that other animals need to survive. Read this book to find out how animals rely on elephants to maintain the savanna.

WEBSITES

The Elephant Listening Project
http://www.birds.cornell.edu/brp/elephant/
The Elephant Listening Project's website provides up-to-date information of the scientists' work, information on forest elephants, and video interviews with Katy and Peter.

ELP Rumbles
https://medium.com/elp-rumbles
The Elephant Listening Project's blog, written by Cornell student volunteers, includes articles about biodiversity in the forest, new research on forest elephants, and poaching updates.

"60 Minutes Presents: Secret Language of Elephants"
https://www.youtube.com/watch?v=owXlAQ4-4o0
Watch a fifteen-minute interview with Andrea Turkalo on "60 Minutes Presents: Secret Language of Elephants." She takes the CBS news crew to Dzanga Bai, and you will see her camp, the mirador and, of course, elephants!

INDEX

PHOTO ACKNOWLEDGMENTS

Images: © Elephant Listening Project.

Sound and Video Files: © Elephant Listening Project.

Additional images: Marylia/Shutterstock.com (elephant shape); VanReeel/Shutterstock.com (QR code background); Courtesy of Katy Payne, pp. 7, 13; Terry Oakley/Alamy Stock Photo, p. 8; Anan Kaewkhammul/Shutterstock.com, p. 9; Courtesy of the author, p. 10 (right); Laura Westlund/Independent Picture Service, pp. 11, 18; Nigel Pavitt/John Warburton-Lee Photography Ltd/AWL Images/Getty Images, p. 12; © Andrea Turkalo/Elephant Listening Project, pp. 16, 19 (right), 21, 22, 24, 31, 34, 41, 49; Michael Gottschalk/Photothek/Getty Images, p. 17; © Nicolas Bout/Elephant Listening Project, p. 37; Courtesy Anahita Verehrami, p. 39; ANDREYGUDKOV/iStock/Getty Images Plus/Getty Images, p. 42; Michael Gottschalk/Photothek/Getty Images, p. 46; Courtesy of Taegen Yardley, p. 50.

Cover: © Andrea Turkalo/Elephant Listening Project; Roger de la Harpe/Gallo Images/Getty Images; Anan Kaewkhammul/Shutterstock.com.